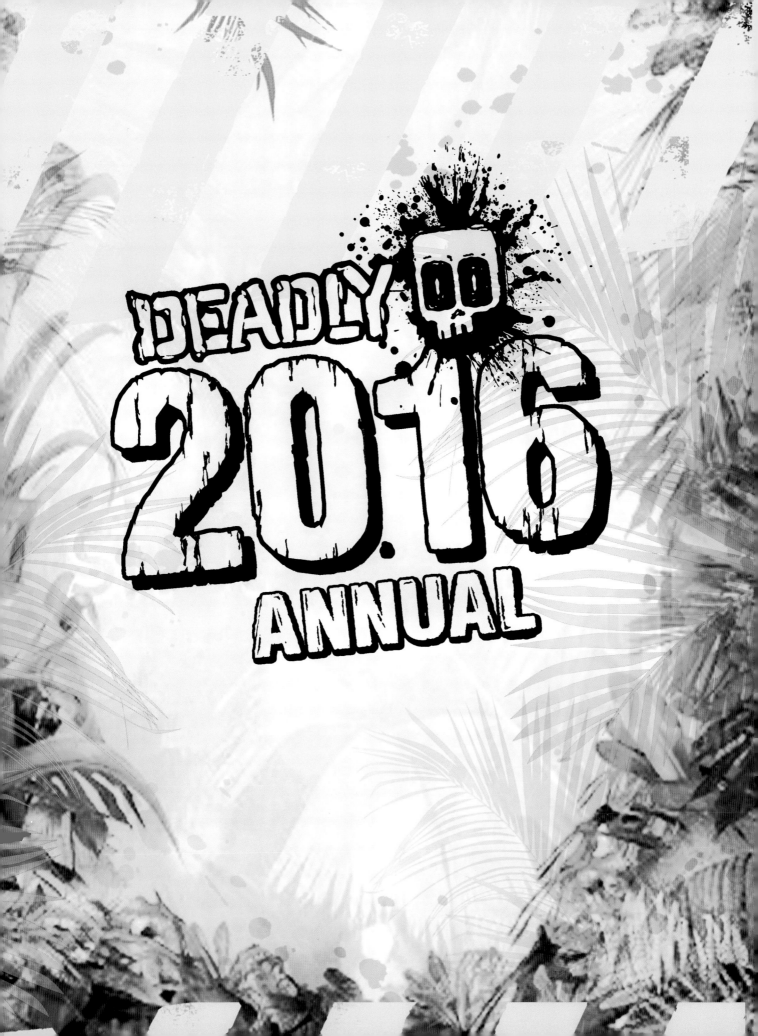

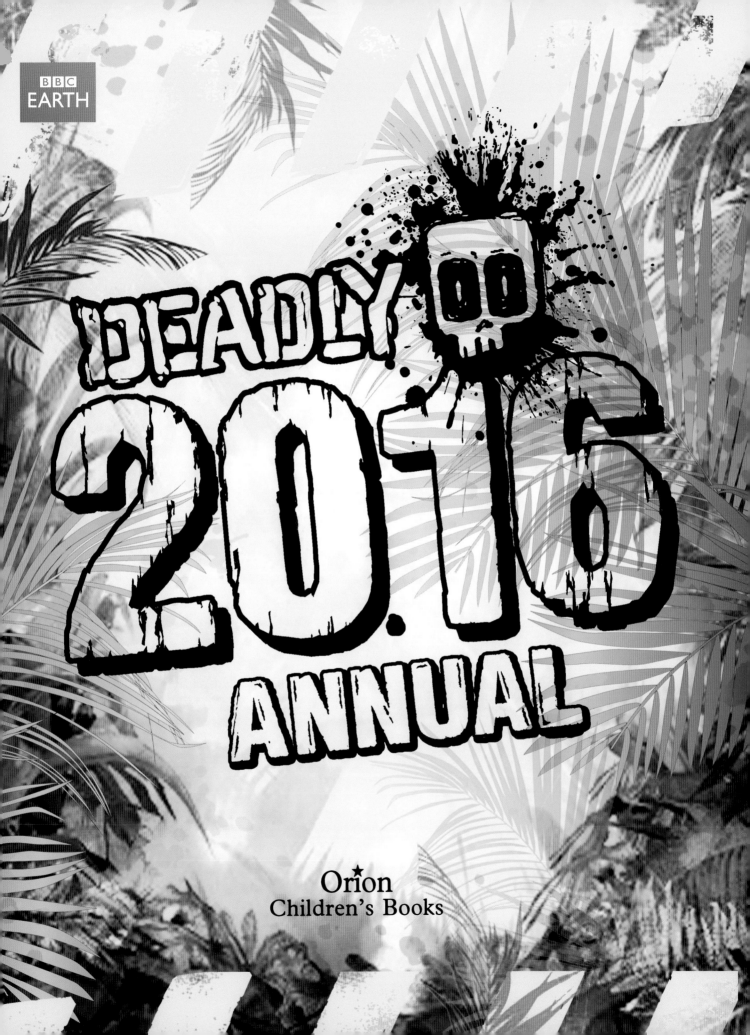

First published in Great Britain in 2015
by Orion Children's Books
An imprint of Hachette Children's Group
Part of Hodder & Stoughton
Carmelite House
50 Victoria Embankment
London EC4Y 0DZ
An Hachette UK Company

PHOTO CREDITS (b: bottom; t: top: l: left; r: right; c: centre)

BBC: 6 Katy Elson 2012 (from Deadly 60 Series 3); 11 Katy Elson 2012 (from Deadly 60 Series 3); 24br James Brickell 2009 (from Deadly 60 Series 1); 27r Kirstine Davidson 2010 (from Deadly 60 Series 2); 32tl Scott Alexander 2010 (from Deadly 60 Series 2); 60 Ruth Harries 2010 (from Deadly 60 Series 2); 72 Ruth Harries 2012 (from Deadly 60 Series 3). **iStock:** 44bl GlobalP; 44c GlobalP; 44bl GlobalP; 57tr Matt Gibson; 65tl GlobalP; 65tr GlobalP. **NaturePL.com/BBC:** 26-27 Andy Rouse. **Shutterstock:** 12-13 Alan Poulson Photography; 14t Brian Lasenby; 14b Worldswildlifewonders; 15t Robert Eastman; 15b Cathy Keifer; 16tl Eric Isselee; 16tr Teguh Tirtaputra; 16b Rich Carey; 16cr Marco Uliana; 18 Visceralimage; 19 Frank L Junior; 22t SekarB; 22b Dmytro Pylypenko; 23b Ivan Kuzmin; 24t Ecoprint; 28-29 Mycteria; 30tl Zstock; 30br D. Kucharski/K Kucharska; 31tl D. Kucharski/K Kucharska; 31bl Iceink; 31br Leela Sae-ang; 32tr Willyam Bradberry; 34 Kirsten Wahiquist; 35 Pyma; 36-37 Nagel Photography; 38tr Eric Isselee; 38-39 Ciaffra; 40t Reptiles4all; 40c Worldswildlifewonders; 42 Sylvia Bouchard; 43 Incredible Arctic; 44tr Imageman; 45t Laurent Renault; 45b Brian Lasenby; 48t Fenkieandreas; 48b Ricardo Reitmeyer; 49tl WithGod; 49tr Javarman; 49b Skydie; 50c Mogens Trolle; 50br Kurt_G; 52 Butterfly Hunter; 53 Wong Yu Liang; 54-55 Matthew Cole; 56 Patrick K Cambell; 57tl Chepe Nicoli; 57 Eduard Kynlynskyy; 58t Efendy; 58b John Michael Evan Potter; 64tl Yusran Abdul Rahman; 66tr Cyhel; 66c James Van der Broek; 66br Matts9122; 68 Craig Burrows; 70 Angel Dibilio; 71t Michiel de Wit; 71b Lindsay Basson. **Thinkstock:** 20-21 Naluphoto; 23tr Natasha Litova; 24bl FtLaudGirl; 38tl StockPhotoAstur; 39t Wendi Evans; 39b Vladoskan; 40br Fuse; 46-47 Amanda Cotton; 50tr Amanda Cotton; 61 Mogens Trolle; 62-63 & 64br Ginophotos; 65 reptiles4all; 69 GlobalP.

Compiled by Jinny Johnson
Designed by Sue Michniewicz

A CIP catalogue record for this book is available from the British Library.

ISBN 978 1 5101 0001 5

2 4 6 8 10 9 7 5 3 1

Printed and bound in Germany

www.orionchildrens.co.uk
www.hachette.co.uk

MIX
Paper from
responsible sources
FSC® C011124

CONTENTS

WELCOME

TO THE 2016 DEADLY ANNUAL!

Hello, Deadly fans. In our latest annual we want to tell you more about how some of the world's most successful predators catch their prey. Many rely on fast running, swimming or flying. Others have super-sharp teeth, claws or other weapons, while some rely on powerful venomous bites. There are also hunters that play cunning tricks on their victims and even a few animals that use sticks and stones to help them bag their meal.

Find out more about these incredible creatures and enjoy loads of pictures and puzzles, as well as a Deadly quiz. Have fun!

CHAPTER 1
DEADLY TRICKS

Not all **predators**

depend on **strength** and **sharp** teeth

to **catch** their prey.

Some have some very **clever** ways

of tempting their **victims** to come

dangerously close, then they **attack**.

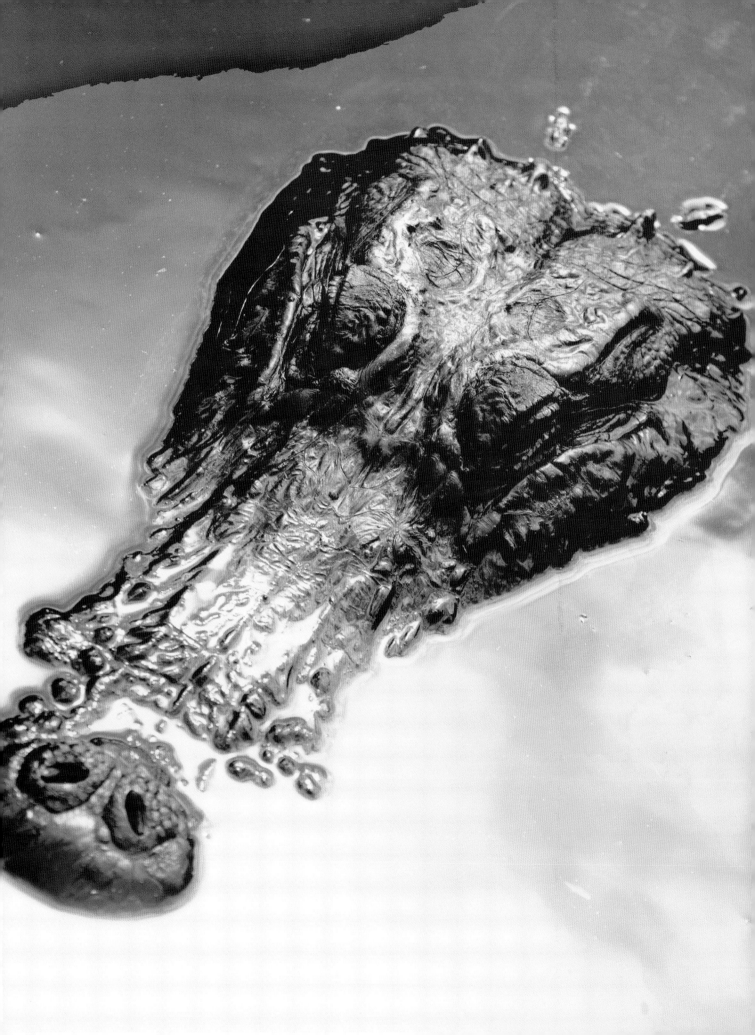

DEADLY TRICKS FACTS

Fishermen use bait to help them catch fish – and so does the **GREEN HERON**. This long-legged bird wades in rivers and ponds searching for prey. To attract the fish, the heron often drops insects or other things it finds on the riverbank, such as twigs or even bits of bread, into the water. When the fish arrive to investigate, the heron snatches them up with its dagger-like beak.

The **MARGAY** is a wild cat which lives in Central and South America. In its forest home its patterned coat helps it stay hidden from prey and larger predators.

Like all cats, the margay is a skilful hunter. Scientists recently observed margays playing a sly trick to catch tamarins – a kind of small monkey. The margay spotted tamarins feeding in a tree and, after hiding in vines nearby, started making a sound very like the call of a baby tamarin. The adult tamarins became curious and climbed close to where the margay was hiding. When they got close enough, the margay pounced – clever cat!

FIREFLIES are actually a kind of beetle and not flies at all. They fly at night and they can make light in their own bodies. They use this light to attract one another in a sequence of flashes, and each species has its own pattern of flashes.

But one kind of firefly, *Photuris*, plays a nasty trick to get a meal. The female *Photuris* firefly watches out for flashes made by males of another kind of firefly called *Photinus*. When she sees one, she replies, mimicking the signal of female *Photinus* fireflies. When the male comes close, thinking he's found a mate, the *Photuris* female seizes him and gobbles him up!

Some alligators and crocodiles have a crafty way of tempting birds close enough to catch. Wading birds such as egrets and herons often nest around swamps and pools where **AMERICAN ALLIGATORS** live. In the breeding season all the birds are busy collecting lots of twigs and sticks to make their nests, and the alligator takes advantage of this.

The alligator lurks in the water with a stick lying across its snout. The bird approaches to snatch the stick – but then the alligator's jaws snap open and grab the bird before it can fly away. Mugger crocodiles in India may also hunt this way.

The **CANTIL** is a deadly pit viper which preys on other reptiles as well as on birds and mammals. It has long fangs to deliver lethal wounds to its victims. A full-grown cantil can be to 1.3 metres long and is powerful enough to tackle a wide range of prey.

The **WOBBEGONG SHARK** has a fleshy fringe around its mouth. If another fish comes close to investigate it gets snapped up in seconds.

A young cantil has a bright yellow tip to its tail, which it wiggles as it lies in wait for prey. Frogs and lizards see this movement and come close, hoping for a mouthful of tasty caterpillar or worm, only to be met by the cantil's fangs. As the cantil grows, its bright tail fades to dark brown or black like the rest of its body.

Insects can play tricks too. The **ASSASSIN BUG** likes to feed on spiders. It creeps up to a web and plucks at the silken threads to make them vibrate. The spider thinks it has a victim and comes to investigate. But instead of enjoying its meal, the spider is quickly stabbed by the assassin bug's sharp snout.

Other creatures play similar tricks to the young cantils. The death adder wiggles its tail to attract hungry birds and other animals. And the **FROGFISH** (a kind of anglerfish) has a lure above its mouth which other fish think might be a tempting morsel.

DEADLY TRICKS WORDSEARCH

All these animals use clever tricks to help them catch
their prey. Can you find their names in this wordsearch puzzle?

R	N	U	T	T	M	W	V	M	P	U	N	G	R	H
E	F	O	W	W	O	P	A	E	Y	R	L	K	S	A
D	I	M	R	B	O	R	U	M	N	B	K	I	Z	C
D	R	F	U	E	G	B	J	Z	U	O	F	T	A	B
A	E	B	I	A	H	R	B	T	Z	R	S	N	N	Q
H	F	N	Y	X	Q	N	J	E	E	B	T	F	E	M
T	L	R	S	B	A	X	E	L	G	I	A	K	L	S
A	Y	P	Z	C	R	Y	G	E	L	O	F	Q	M	M
E	D	T	O	D	U	N	H	V	R	B	N	U	Q	I
D	B	M	S	Z	A	A	I	D	I	G	W	G	O	I
R	E	G	D	A	B	P	Q	H	F	Q	F	O	W	T
S	H	L	M	E	E	A	L	L	I	G	A	T	O	R
J	R	G	E	R	W	B	N	K	K	A	A	Q	N	M
G	U	B	N	I	S	S	A	S	S	A	O	R	O	Y
S	V	Q	R	D	G	W	T	T	Z	Z	P	R	Y	B

MARGAY **BADGER** **ANGLERFISH** **ASSASSIN BUG**
GREEN HERON **ALLIGATOR** **CANTIL VIPER** **WOBBEGONG**
FIREFLY **DEATH ADDER**

17

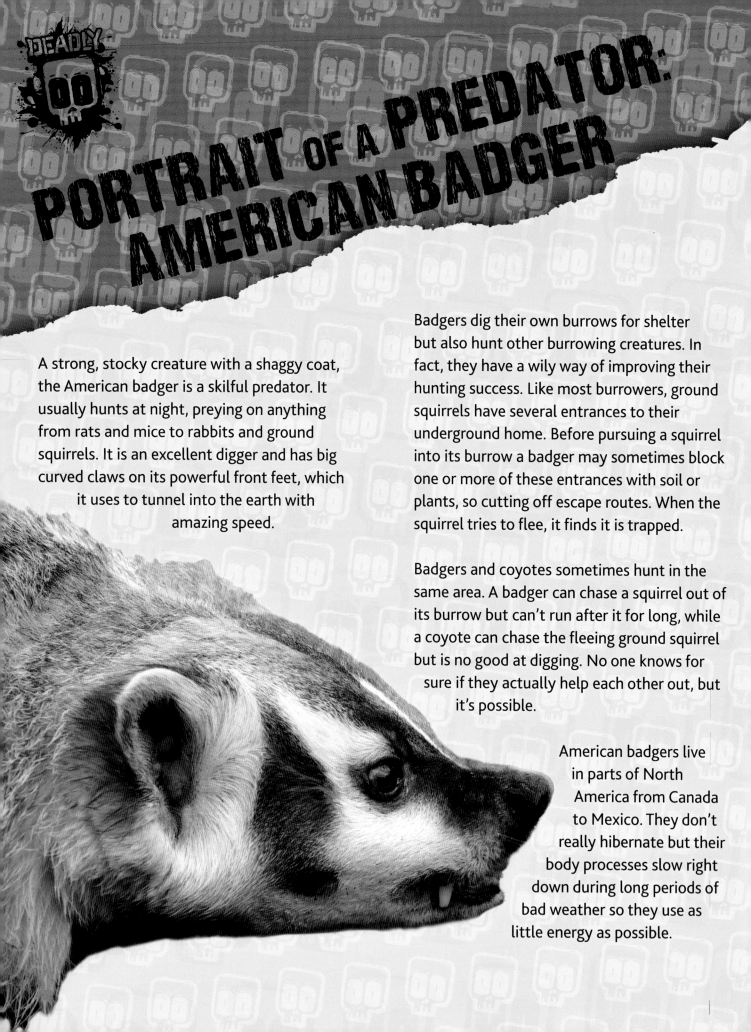

PORTRAIT OF A PREDATOR: AMERICAN BADGER

A strong, stocky creature with a shaggy coat, the American badger is a skilful predator. It usually hunts at night, preying on anything from rats and mice to rabbits and ground squirrels. It is an excellent digger and has big curved claws on its powerful front feet, which it uses to tunnel into the earth with amazing speed.

Badgers dig their own burrows for shelter but also hunt other burrowing creatures. In fact, they have a wily way of improving their hunting success. Like most burrowers, ground squirrels have several entrances to their underground home. Before pursuing a squirrel into its burrow a badger may sometimes block one or more of these entrances with soil or plants, so cutting off escape routes. When the squirrel tries to flee, it finds it is trapped.

Badgers and coyotes sometimes hunt in the same area. A badger can chase a squirrel out of its burrow but can't run after it for long, while a coyote can chase the fleeing ground squirrel but is no good at digging. No one knows for sure if they actually help each other out, but it's possible.

American badgers live in parts of North America from Canada to Mexico. They don't really hibernate but their body processes slow right down during long periods of bad weather so they use as little energy as possible.

Stripy face

Size: 42–72 centimetres long
with a tail of 10–16 centimetres

Large front feet
with curved claws
for digging

Short but strong legs

19

CHAPTER 2
DEADLY SPEED

The **animals** in this chapter are all supreme **speedsters**, able to **run**, **fly** or swim **faster** than their **prey**. And most can **beat** any human speed **records**.

DEADLY SPEED FACTS

The **GENTOO PENGUIN** is one of the fastest swimming birds, clocking up an amazing 35 kilometres an hour over short distances. Olympic champion Michael Phelps is one of the fastest human swimmers ever, but even he can only manage 6–7 kilometres an hour.

Like all penguins, the gentoo has wings but cannot fly. Instead it uses its wings like flippers to power through the water and its webbed feet to help it steer. The gentoo can also dive to over 150 metres as it chases fishy prey.

The ostrich is the fastest bird on land and can run at 72 kilometres an hour, but it cannot fly. The fastest-running flying bird is the **ROADRUNNER**, which can race along at up to 42 kilometres an hour as it hunts in the desert for insects, lizards and snakes. Many of its prey are speedy movers too, so the roadrunner has to be able to overtake them. The roadrunner is a member of the cuckoo family and about 50–60 centimetres long.

How fast do you think insects can run? Cockroaches are fast movers but the **AUSTRALIAN TIGER BEETLE** is probably the insect speed champion. It runs at about 2.5 metres a second (9 kilometres an hour) as it hunts other beetles, ants and caterpillars.

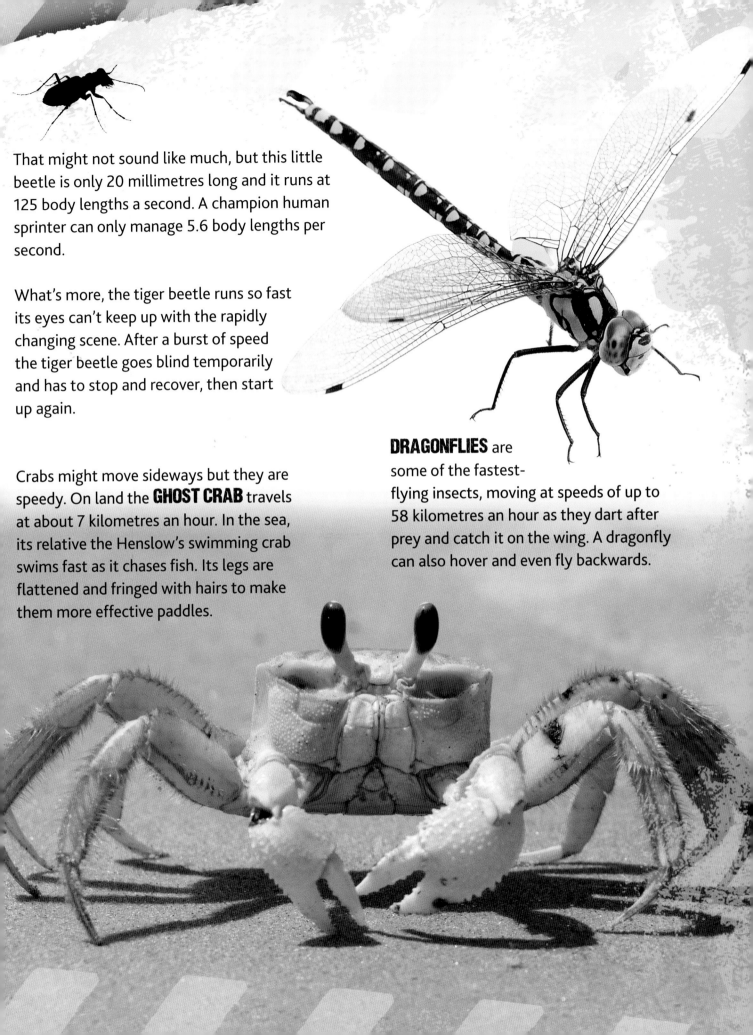

That might not sound like much, but this little beetle is only 20 millimetres long and it runs at 125 body lengths a second. A champion human sprinter can only manage 5.6 body lengths per second.

What's more, the tiger beetle runs so fast its eyes can't keep up with the rapidly changing scene. After a burst of speed the tiger beetle goes blind temporarily and has to stop and recover, then start up again.

Crabs might move sideways but they are speedy. On land the **GHOST CRAB** travels at about 7 kilometres an hour. In the sea, its relative the Henslow's swimming crab swims fast as it chases fish. Its legs are flattened and fringed with hairs to make them more effective paddles.

DRAGONFLIES are some of the fastest-flying insects, moving at speeds of up to 58 kilometres an hour as they dart after prey and catch it on the wing. A dragonfly can also hover and even fly backwards.

Crocodiles are good swimmers and they can also move quickly on land. The **FRESHWATER CROCODILE**, which lives in northern Australia, is particularly fast and gallops along at 17 kilometres an hour.

The **SAILFISH** is one of the most extraordinary-looking fish in the sea and also one of the fastest moving. The fish gets its name from the huge fin that runs along its back and can be extended – like a sail. The sailfish also has a forked tail, a very long upper jaw like a pointed beak, and a sleek, streamlined body.

It's difficult to time the movement of fish, but the sailfish is said to swim at up to 110 kilometres an hour for short distances. Other fish are its main prey, but it also eats squid and octopus.

A full-grown sailfish can reach 3.4 metres in length and weigh as much as 100 kilograms.

The **PEREGRINE FALCON** is the fastest-flying bird, making spectacular dives at an incredible 320 kilometres an hour as it plunges through the air to seize prey.

The eider duck moves fast in level flight. It has been timed flying at speeds of about 76 kilometres an hour.

DEADLY SPEED WORDSEARCH

All these animals are fast movers.
Can you find their names in this wordsearch puzzle?

A	R	G	C	Q	F	F	M	Y	Q	F	E	G	O	H
I	P	E	K	H	G	U	L	P	R	J	N	E	S	I
U	X	X	N	S	E	F	B	I	T	D	I	N	T	V
K	I	B	F	N	N	E	G	C	Y	M	R	T	R	R
V	N	P	W	O	U	A	T	T	N	T	G	O	I	F
S	A	H	G	L	T	R	X	A	A	J	E	O	C	N
E	W	A	I	E	M	N	D	W	H	G	R	P	H	F
B	R	O	B	L	C	X	K	A	J	L	E	E	E	C
D	N	I	D	W	Q	O	J	K	O	P	P	N	F	B
X	R	B	K	E	L	T	E	E	B	R	E	G	I	T
D	C	S	A	I	L	F	I	S	H	F	W	U	W	I
W	E	K	K	P	E	U	G	P	C	T	M	I	O	G
O	N	I	E	O	I	R	O	D	Z	G	E	N	A	C
V	A	E	V	Z	T	V	U	Q	M	U	L	E	P	M
R	B	D	X	P	C	N	E	S	V	B	R	D	C	F

PEREGRINE   **CHEETAH**   **OSTRICH**   **GENTOO PENGUIN**
FRIGATE BIRD   **LION**   **DRAGONFLY**   **ROADRUNNER**
SAILFISH   **TIGER BEETLE**

PORTRAIT OF A PREDATOR: CHEETAH

Over short distances the cheetah wins the land speed contest every time. It can run at up to 87 kilometres an hour – but can only keep up that pace for a few hundred metres. The cheetah needs to move fast to catch speedy prey such as Thomson's gazelle, which can travel at 64 kilometres an hour and also make bounding leaps to avoid predators. When hunting, a cheetah carefully stalks its prey, getting as close as it can before starting to run. If the cheetah does manage to overtake, it usually

Small head

Flexible spine

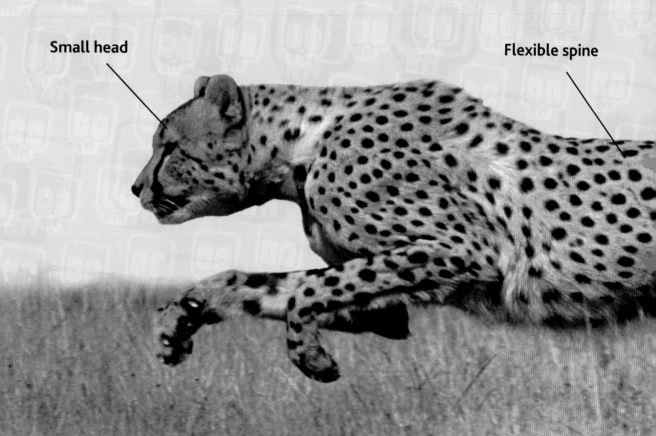

knocks its victim to the ground, then goes for the throat to deliver a killing bite.

Long legs and a very flexible spine, which curves up and down during running, help the cheetah's speed. Also, while most cats have retractable claws, which means they are held back in protective sheaths, the cheetah's claws are not fully retractable and act like spiked running shoes to help it grip. A long tail helps the cheetah keep its balance during its high-speed chases. This cat also has large nostrils, allowing it to take in extra air.

Cheetahs live on grassy plains and open woodland in Africa. There are also a small number of cheetahs in Iran.

Size: up to 1.3 metres long with a tail of 66–84 centimetres

Slender body

Long legs

27

Some **animals**, including many **spiders**, use traps to catch their **prey**. Making the **trap** can take a bit of **effort** but then the predator can **sit** by and wait for **meals** to come its way. A **few**

creatures make use of **tools** such as sticks and **stones** to help them obtain a **meal**. Some animals use tools in **non-deadly** ways. **Octopus** have been seen gathering coconut shells and using them as **shelters** to **protect** themselves from predators!

DEADLY TRAPS & TOOLS FACTS

The **WATER SPIDER** really does live and hunt in the water, but it has to have a supply of air. First it spins a special silken web that looks like a bubble and attaches this to water plants. Then it goes back to the surface, where it traps tiny bubbles of air on the hairs on its body and takes these down to the underwater web. It makes several trips until its home is well stocked with air.

Then the spider settles down to watch for prey. When it spots something it pounces and pulls the victim into its bubble web where it can be enjoyed in safety.

The **TRAPDOOR SPIDER** is a relative of the tarantulas but smaller and less hairy. It spends much of its life in a burrow, which doubles as a safe shelter and an amazingly efficient trap for catching prey.

The spider digs the burrow using the special rake-like structures on its jaws, and lines it with silk. The door of the burrow has silken hinges and opens and closes very quickly and easily. The door is covered with bits of moss, leaves and twigs so it's very hard for any passing insect to spot.

This door is also surrounded with silken strands spreading out over the ground. If any passing insect disturbs these strands, the trapdoor spider senses the vibrations. It rushes out of the burrow, grabs its prey and is back inside with its meal in no time.

30

The best known of all animal traps are made by **GARDEN SPIDERS**. We see their beautiful silken webs every day and they are amazingly effective for catching prey.

The spider makes its distinctive orb web with silk spun from its own body. It starts by attaching strands of silk to supports such as plants to make a frame. It adds spokes, then spins a spiral of sticky silk to trap flying insects. The finished web can measure as much as 40 centimetres across.

Once its web is complete, the spider sits at the centre or nearby, watching for prey. When an unwary insect flies into the web the spider quickly bites it, then wraps it in silk to prevent escape. The spider can then eat its meal at its leisure.

The adult **ANTLION** looks rather like a damselfly with long delicate wings. But its young (larvae) look very different. They are fierce predators and have huge curved jaws for attacking other insects. The name 'antlion' actually refers to these larvae, not the adults.

The young antlion catches its prey in a special trap. It digs a funnel-shaped pit in fine, sandy soil and settles down at the bottom to wait. It may be half buried in the sand, with only its ferocious jaws showing.

If a passing ant or other insect tumbles into the pit and tries to struggle out, the antlion hurls more sand at it, making it impossible for the victim to escape. The prey soon sinks down to the bottom of the pit into the antlion's waiting jaws. The antlion pierces the prey's body and sucks out its body fluids. It then tosses the remains out of the pit and gets ready for the next victim to come along.

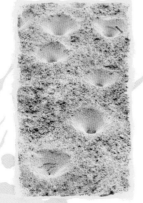

Humans aren't the only animals that find sponges useful! **BOTTLENOSE DOLPHINS** have been seen wearing bits of sea sponge on their nose as they search the sea floor for food. The sponge may protect the dolphin's sensitive nose from spiky poisonous creatures, and also helps to stir up fish hidden in the sand. Most of the dolphins seen using sponges in this way have been females and it seems that they pass the skill on to their young.

Ostrich eggs are a favourite food of the **EGYPTIAN VULTURE**, but these eggs are large – weighing as much 1.3 kilograms – and their shells are thick. To break the shell, the vulture picks up a stone in its beak and hurls it at the egg. It may take several blows before the egg is cracked enough for the vulture to get its beak in there and swallow the contents. Egyptian vultures have also been seen dropping stones on to eggs from the air.

Did you know that sponges are actually very simple animals? They live by filtering small particles of food from the water.

CHIMPANZEES have been seen using more kinds of tools and in more different ways than any animal other than humans. Chimps drop branches or throw objects to warn off attackers. They also use sticks and stones to obtain food. For instance, a chimp will poke a stick into a termite mound to pull out some tasty insects, or smash nut shells with rocks.

Orangutans also use tools such as sticks to collect insects and honey.

TRAPS & TOOLS WORDSEARCH

These animals all use traps or tools to help them bag a meal
or to protect themselves. Can you find their names in this puzzle?

P	Y	B	Y	V	B	P	S	D	K	E	O	I	P	O
Y	R	C	T	V	E	J	F	U	T	T	A	M	R	S
W	E	O	C	T	J	A	J	I	P	S	Y	E	Y	X
F	D	R	G	H	S	O	K	E	M	O	D	B	F	A
V	I	A	T	L	I	V	E	Q	C	I	T	Z	H	Q
I	P	N	T	W	R	M	E	O	P	S	T	C	I	U
L	S	G	G	N	B	H	P	S	E	Z	U	H	O	S
E	R	U	T	L	U	V	N	A	I	T	P	Y	G	E
L	O	T	L	I	W	E	O	M	N	G	R	Y	I	G
C	O	A	Q	R	D	T	T	J	R	Z	D	T	W	I
A	D	N	R	R	T	N	B	Y	X	J	E	M	O	F
Q	P	R	A	E	N	O	I	L	T	N	A	E	R	C
Y	A	G	R	Z	J	J	Z	K	H	L	C	K	Q	C	S
S	R	O	K	Y	I	A	J	G	M	Q	L	N	G	V
N	T	J	W	A	T	E	R	S	P	I	D	E	R	P

SEA OTTER   **WATER SPIDER**   **OCTOPUS**   **EGYPTIAN VULTURE**
CHIMPANZEE   **GARDEN SPIDER**   **ORANGUTAN**   **TRAPDOOR SPIDER**
ANTLION   **CROW**

33

PORTRAIT OF A PREDATOR: SEA OTTER

Sea otters might look cute and cuddly but they are deadly hunters, with a special way of opening hard-shelled sea creatures.

The sea otter lives in the northern Pacific Ocean and spends nearly all its life in the sea. It has amazingly thick fur to keep it warm in the cold water – in fact, it has the thickest coat of any mammal, with about 100,000 hairs per square centimetre. Its broad back feet are

webbed and they act like flippers to help the animal power through the ocean.

Clams, mussels and sea urchins are the sea otter's favourite food, but their shells can be difficult to open. When the sea otter dives for food it often picks up a stone as well – it has little pouches under its armpits for storing its finds. When it surfaces, the sea otter lies on its back in the water with the stone on its chest and pounds the mussel or clam against it until it cracks open. The otter can then feast on the juicy flesh inside. Otters have also been seen using bits of wood, glass, cans and other objects thrown away by humans to pound their prey.

Despite its warm coat, the sea otter still needs lots of food to help it keep warm in the chilly Pacific waters, and it has to eat about a quarter of its body weight every day.

Size: up to 1.48 metres long and 45 kilograms in weight

Webbed back feet

Sharp teeth

Strong tail

CHAPTER 4
DEADLY SENSES

Super senses of **sight**, **hearing** and **smell** help predators track down their **prey**.

Some also have **extra-special** senses such as the **ability** to 'see' **heat** in the **dark** or pick up tiny **electrical** signals given off by **prey**.

DEADLY SENSES FACTS

Birds of prey need excellent eyesight so they can search out prey as they soar high in the air, then swoop down to catch it. The fast-flying **PEREGRINE FALCON** is believed to have vision that's eight times better than ours, and to be able to spot prey more than 3 kilometres away.

Another bird that uses its sense of smell to find food is the New Zealand **KIWI**. The kiwi cannot fly and finds all its food on the ground. It uses the nostrils at the end of its long slender beak to discover creatures such as worms and slugs hiding among dead leaves on the ground.

Most birds don't have a very good sense of smell – they rely more on sight for finding prey. But **TURKEY VULTURES** are different. They feed mostly on animals that are already dead and use smell to help them sniff out a possible meal, even when flying over dense forest. They very rarely kill their own prey.

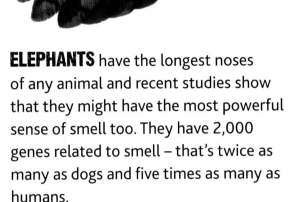

ELEPHANTS have the longest noses of any animal and recent studies show that they might have the most powerful sense of smell too. They have 2,000 genes related to smell – that's twice as many as dogs and five times as many as humans.

Elephants don't have very good eyesight and may use smell to help them find food, pick up the scent of enemies and find their way around.

BARN OWLS have excellent hearing. They usually hunt at dusk and dawn in very low light so have to rely on the slightest sound to track down prey. The owl's ears are hidden under feathers at each side of its head and one is positioned slightly higher than the other. This helps the owl work out exactly where a sound is coming from. Its ears are particularly sensitive to the sounds made by small animals such as rodents.

A barn owl also flies very quietly so the sound of its own movement doesn't distract it. Its wing feathers have soft edges so make less sound as they move through the air.

SHARKS use their incredible sense of smell to help them find prey in the ocean. They can smell a tiny amount of blood in the water from as much as 5 kilometres away.

Some animals have special senses that we just don't have. **PIT VIPERS**, for instance, are able to hunt at night because they can 'see' the heat given off by a prey's body. The snake has little holes on each side of the face near the eyes. These are called pit organs and can pick up heat given off by an animal, creating a kind of thermal picture for the snake.

The **PLATYPUS** shelters in a riverside burrow during the day, but at night it comes out and slips into the water to hunt shellfish, worms and insect larvae. To find its prey in a muddy riverbed, it uses its curious duck-like beak, which is equipped with lots of special electric receptors. These pick up the tiniest pulses of electricity given off by moving prey and allow the platypus to home in on its meal.

SEALS use their sensitive whiskers to track down prey in the ocean. These whiskers detect movements in the water made by a swimming fish. Scientists believe a seal may be able to work out the size and shape of the fish from the sensations it picks up with its whiskers.

DEADLY SENSES WORDSEARCH

All these animals have super senses to help them find food and avoid danger. Can you find their names in this puzzle?

E	P	M	E	O	G	W	R	L	R	T	G	F	D	A
V	R	I	R	G	E	Y	R	K	A	O	O	E	X	U
P	A	U	T	W	B	K	B	Y	E	O	N	A	C	L
Q	O	S	T	V	D	F	C	L	B	I	Y	W	C	V
X	V	X	P	L	I	I	K	P	R	H	I	S	D	V
M	K	H	P	U	U	P	R	G	A	Q	W	M	O	P
H	G	R	O	U	O	V	E	V	L	S	U	N	G	L
Q	T	R	A	Y	E	R	Y	R	O	V	O	R	Y	A
J	A	Y	J	H	E	Q	X	E	P	K	E	V	C	T
X	L	X	I	P	S	E	A	I	K	Y	A	L	P	Y
L	W	O	N	R	A	B	V	D	S	R	N	D	W	P
G	P	X	Y	D	E	U	T	E	N	U	U	Q	I	U
B	G	E	L	E	P	H	A	N	T	W	M	T	W	S
N	M	D	R	P	T	L	D	O	N	K	K	H	I	D
M	K	T	R	K	N	A	A	C	K	P	T	S	K	I

POLAR BEAR   SHARK   ELEPHANT   PLATYPUS

KIWI   BARN OWL   PIT VIPER   GREY SEAL

PEREGRINE   TURKEY VULTURE

PORTRAIT OF A PREDATOR: POLAR BEAR

Polar bears live in the Arctic where food is hard to come by and they often have to travel great distances to find food. Fortunately, a polar bear has an amazing sense of smell and can sniff out prey from a kilometre away. It can even smell animals hidden under a metre of snow.

The polar bear is one of the largest of all land predators and it feeds only on meat. Seals are its main prey, but it also hunts birds, walruses and even small whales. It may stalk its prey on the ice or lie in wait for a seal to pop up at a breathing hole. The polar bear's sense of smell also allows it to detect baby seals in dens under the snow.

Polar bears can run on land for short distances and are expert swimmers, using their large front paws as paddles. They can swim at about 6.5 kilometres an hour and can keep going for distances of 65 kilometres or more across open water. Their thick fur and layer of fat keeps them warm in the cold Arctic sea. If food is scarce, the polar bear can slow down its body processes so it uses as little energy as possible, and can go for many weeks without eating.

Size: up to 2.6 metres long and 600 kilograms in weight

Thick coat

Strong legs and broad feet

Rough soles of feet to help grip on ice

FIGHTING BACK:

Predators don't always have an easy time of it. Lots of animals have very effective ways of defending themselves against their enemies – and some of these are quite surprising!

Hungry hunters soon learn to stay well away from **SKUNKS**. If an enemy gets too close and a skunk feels in danger, it turns around and sprays out a very smelly liquid from special glands near its tail. This smells terrible and can hurt the other creature's eyes. The stink takes days to wear off too. After this experience, most predators look for other prey. The skunk can spray the liquid as far as 3 metres.

POTATO BEETLES feed on the leaves of potatoes and other plants in the deadly nightshade family and they also lay eggs on these plants. The young beetles (larvae) make a tasty snack for lots of other creatures, but they have a good way of protecting themselves. They cover their body in their own poo, which makes them very smelly and unappealing to predators.

Some of the most poisonous of all animals are tiny **POISON DART FROGS**, which live in rainforests in Central and South America. The poison is contained in the frog's skin and can kill or paralyse anything that tries to eat it. There are lots of different kinds of poison dart frog and all are very colourful. Their bright colours and patterns are a warning to predators to stay well away, or else!

DEADLY DEFENCES

The **WHITE RHINOCEROS** is one of the world's biggest land animals. It is a plant eater and spends most of its time quietly munching grasses, but if a rhino gets angry it is a fearsome beast. It has two horns on its huge head and will use these to defend itself against attackers or to protect young. The largest horns can grow up to 1.5 metres long, and a blow from a charging rhino can do serious damage to an enemy.

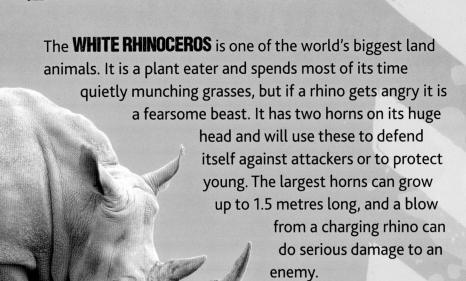

The little **HORNED LIZARD** lives in the desert in the southwestern United States, where it feeds mostly on ants. The lizard's spiky body puts off many predators, as it looks like an awkward mouthful to swallow. But if an attacker does persist, the lizard can squirt blood at its enemy from special ducts at the corners of its eyes.

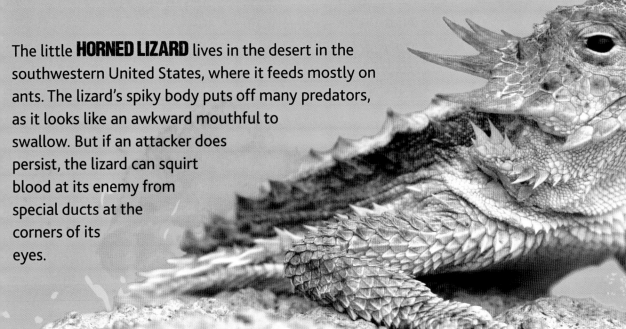

CHAPTER 5
DEADLY WEAPONS

Predators have a range of **deadly** weapons to **help** them catch their **prey**. Many kill with their **teeth** or their **claws** but others **sting** or punch their victims, while some **create** their **own electric** shocks.

DEADLY WEAPONS FACTS

The **PEACOCK MANTIS SHRIMP**'s deadly weapons are its club-like arms, which it uses to deliver a knock-out blow that accelerates faster than a .22 calibre bullet. This shrimp is only 15 centimetres long but its powerful punch moves 50 times faster than we can blink. With this, the shrimp can smash its way into crab and mollusc shells, then feast on the soft flesh inside.

Sharp teeth and strong claws up to 7.5 centimetres long are the **LION**'s main weapons. A lion cannot run fast for very long so it depends on getting close to its prey before bringing it down with a mighty swipe of an immensely powerful paw. It then seizes the prey by the throat with its teeth and holds on until the victim suffocates and dies.

Most of the time the claws are held back in special sheaths to protect them and keep them sharp for those killing moments.

One of the most powerful of all predators, the **GOLDEN EAGLE** kills with its huge, strong feet. It has superb eyesight, which allows it to spot prey such as hares, rabbits and birds as it soars high above the ground. It then dives down at lightning speed to seize its meal in talons tipped with long curved claws. Few animals can escape the eagle's powerful grip. The eagle tears prey apart with its sharp hooked beak.

The **COMMON WASP** has a sharp sting at the end of its brightly striped yellow and black body. The sting has two sharp points and is linked to a venom gland so when the wasp plunges its sting into its victim, venom flows into the wound. The wasp can pull the sting out and use it again.

Wasps use their sting to kill and paralyse prey but they also need it to defend themselves against enemies. Birds and other creatures learn to see black and yellow stripes as a warning and stay well clear.

The **AYE-AYE** lives only on the island of Madagascar and is one of the strangest looking of all primates – the group of animals to which monkeys and chimps also belong. It is active at night and has large ears and huge yellowish eyes.

Its most curious features are its hands. Its slender fingers are tipped with claws and the middle finger on each hand is particularly long and thin. The aye-aye likes to feast on insects and taps on branches and tree trunks to disturb prey living underneath the bark. Once it hears the slightest sound of movement, the aye-aye tears a hole in the wood with its strong teeth, then inserts an extra-long finger to pull out its meal.

The **ELECTRIC EEL** lives in muddy rivers and streams in the Amazon rainforest and has a very unusual way of killing its prey – it gives them an electric shock. Inside this fish's body are specially adapted muscles that release high-voltage charges into the water. These are strong enough to stun or kill other fish and can even give a severe shock to a human.

Electric eels grow to about 2.5 metres long. They also use small electrical pulses to find their way in the water and detect prey.

The **TIGER SHARK** is a fearsome hunter and has extremely strong jaws and teeth. The teeth are very serrated – that means they have jagged edges similar to those on a bread knife – and the shark uses a saw-like action to cut into its prey like a can-opener. Tiger sharks are well known for eating almost anything they can find, including tough-shelled sea turtles.

AFRICAN ELEPHANTS are plant eaters so their tusks are not used against prey. But they do make powerful weapons for fighting off predators, such as big cats, and for use in battles with rival elephants and they can do serious damage. An elephant also uses its tusks for digging up plants and stripping bark from trees to eat.

Both male and female African elephants have tusks. They are actually extra-long front teeth and they keep on growing throughout the elephant's life. The largest known tusk measured an incredible 3.5 metres.

The **TRAP-JAW ANT** might be tiny but it has jaws to rival those of a shark or a hyena. It snaps its super-strong jaws shut at a speed of up to 64 metres a second, or more than 200 kilometres an hour, as it captures prey.

The ant also uses its jaws to stay safe. If it has to escape from an enemy it strikes its jaws on the ground and a latch-like mechanism is triggered to fling the ant into the air and away from danger.

DEADLY WEAPONS WORDSEARCH

The animals in this puzzle all have deadly weapons for attacking prey or defending themselves. Can you find their names?

T	N	A	W	A	J	P	A	R	T	G	X	S	E	T
S	K	S	A	A	B	C	B	I	T	U	I	E	Y	N
G	D	K	H	X	N	N	G	W	E	T	O	L	A	B
E	O	S	O	O	G	E	J	E	N	J	N	E	E	S
A	Q	L	I	S	R	E	T	A	O	H	Y	C	Y	E
B	W	L	D	S	L	J	M	N	P	A	Z	T	A	C
Q	K	H	H	E	Q	G	Q	W	A	Y	Z	R	W	N
F	V	A	M	A	N	T	I	S	S	H	R	I	M	P
Q	R	N	L	I	S	E	R	V	N	L	P	C	R	J
K	S	Z	Y	H	E	N	A	D	H	D	E	E	Y	U
T	X	A	D	E	F	Z	R	G	Q	V	L	E	L	W
Q	R	W	A	S	P	J	N	N	L	A	E	L	F	E
P	K	Y	B	W	W	O	Q	I	X	E	C	A	G	J
O	N	K	G	B	U	R	P	V	C	X	J	K	C	G
P	X	H	T	Y	T	N	Y	F	P	Y	Y	Q	J	W

LION

MANTIS SHRIMP

GOLDEN EAGLE

TIGER SHARK

ELEPHANT

AYE-AYE

WASP

ELECTRIC EEL

PRAYING MANTIS

TRAP-JAW ANT

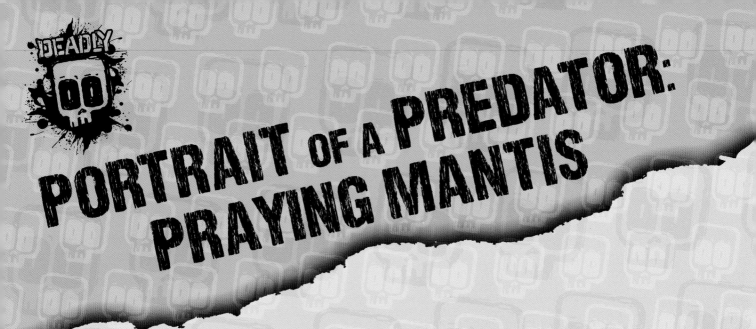

PORTRAIT OF A PREDATOR: PRAYING MANTIS

One of the most efficient of all insect predators, the praying mantis grabs its prey with its fast-moving spiky front legs. As it waits, the mantis holds its deadly killing legs folded neatly together in a pose that looks like someone at prayer – the reason for its name!

The mantis is an ambush hunter and lies in wait on a branch or other perch, watching for prey to come close enough to catch. Many mantids are coloured like leaves, branches or even flowers so they blend into their surroundings and are very hard for prey – or enemies – to see.

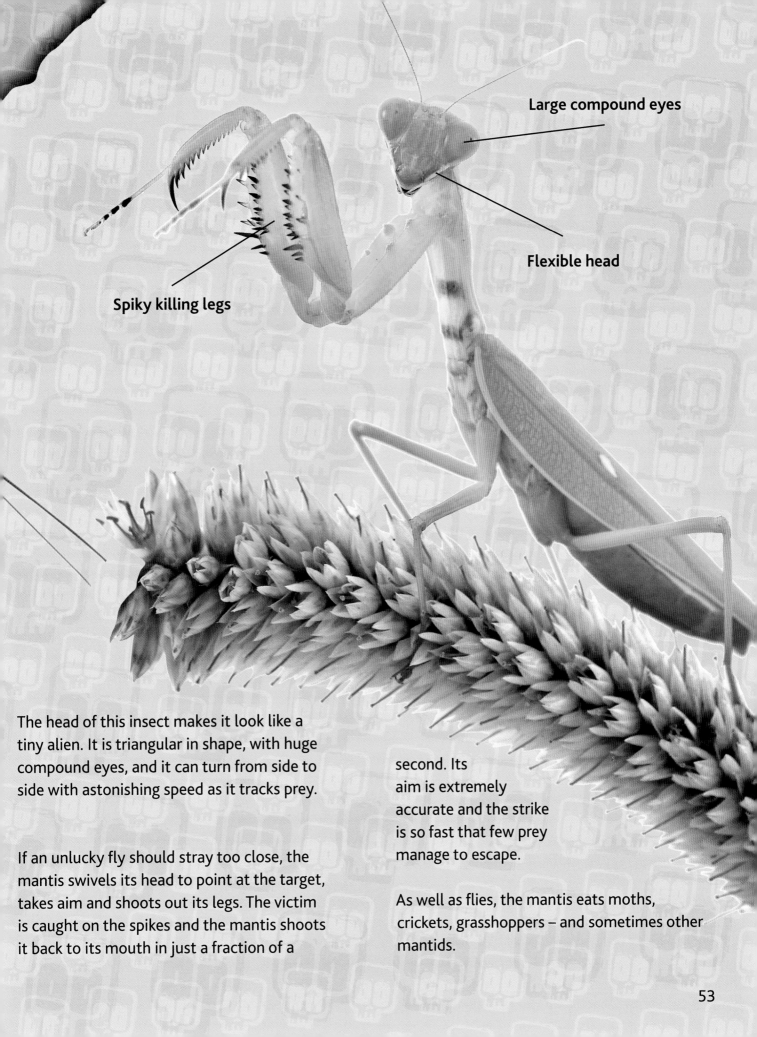

Large compound eyes

Flexible head

Spiky killing legs

The head of this insect makes it look like a tiny alien. It is triangular in shape, with huge compound eyes, and it can turn from side to side with astonishing speed as it tracks prey.

If an unlucky fly should stray too close, the mantis swivels its head to point at the target, takes aim and shoots out its legs. The victim is caught on the spikes and the mantis shoots it back to its mouth in just a fraction of a second. Its aim is extremely accurate and the strike is so fast that few prey manage to escape.

As well as flies, the mantis eats moths, crickets, grasshoppers – and sometimes other mantids.

53

CHAPTER 6
DEADLY POWER & STRENGTH

Some **creatures** are so **strong** and **powerful** it is almost impossible for prey to escape their **clutches**. But, **surprisingly**, one of the strongest animals for its size is a **little** beetle!

DEADLY POWER & STRENGTH FACTS

The **ANACONDA** is the heaviest snake in the world at up to 227 kilograms – that's nearly as much as the weight of four average people. It's not venomous but it is extremely strong and kills its prey with pure power.

Having stealthily crept up on its victim or lain in wait until the prey comes close enough to strike, the anaconda grabs its prey with an array of backward-pointing teeth. It then throws its coils round its victim and squeezes tighter and tighter until the other animal suffocates. The snake's mouth opens very wide, allowing it to swallow prey much larger than its own head. After a big meal, the anaconda won't need to eat for weeks, or even months.

The huge **HARPY EAGLE** lives in tropical rainforests and hunts animals such as monkeys and sloths in the treetops. It is one of the strongest of all birds of prey and the female often carries prey almost half her own weight back to her nest to feed her young. The eagle's claws can be as long as 10 centimetres – as big as the claws of a grizzly bear.

The **JAGUAR** is the biggest cat in the Americas and its jaws may be even more powerful than those of the tiger. Its jaws are so strong that it often kills prey with a bite to the skull between the ears. It can also break the shells of river turtles.

SIBERIAN TIGERS are the biggest of the big cats and males can weigh up to 300 kilograms. Tigers are immensely strong and can tackle prey much larger than themselves – even rhinos and elephants.

One of the strongest creatures of all for its size is the little **DUNG BEETLE**, which is less than 2.5 centimetres long. The beetle collects dung (poo) from animals such as cows and elephants. It makes it into balls and rolls it away to use for the female to lay her eggs in or as food.

These balls of dung can be heavy – many times the weight of the beetle. Scientists have discovered that the strongest dung beetle can move a ball of dung more than a thousand times its own weight. That's like an average person pushing six double-decker buses full of people.

SPOTTED HYENAS are scavengers and feed on leftovers from other predators as well as animals that are already dead. But they are also skilled hunters and packs of hyenas working together can bring down a much bigger animal, such as a wildebeest.

Hyenas have extremely strong jaws and teeth and they can even crunch through bones to gain every bit of nourishment from a carcass. When hyenas have finished their meal, only the prey's horns are left.

POWER & STRENGTH WORDSEARCH

Big or small, all these animals are very strong for their size.
Can you find their names in this puzzle?

H	E	T	X	C	D	K	T	Q	E	G	A	L	F	U
A	N	N	I	O	M	I	H	P	P	N	P	Z	E	I
R	I	G	M	G	D	K	S	L	E	M	Y	L	D	J
P	R	J	R	T	E	F	V	Y	J	A	G	U	A	R
Y	E	B	M	I	N	R	H	K	Y	A	N	K	J	B
E	V	E	C	M	Z	D	A	A	Q	G	U	G	L	M
A	L	C	F	C	E	Z	D	J	B	J	R	B	P	K
G	O	N	S	T	Y	N	L	E	L	M	E	A	G	H
L	W	B	T	H	O	N	E	Y	B	A	D	G	E	R
E	Q	O	V	C	O	T	R	U	B	T	P	F	O	N
L	P	N	A	I	L	L	K	T	J	E	F	Q	P	P
S	R	N	A	E	K	P	R	H	Y	W	A	H	N	G
H	A	I	Q	M	A	Z	K	N	K	T	M	R	H	H
T	X	W	K	D	Q	G	L	R	P	Z	R	V	Q	N
N	A	Z	D	A	W	E	L	I	D	O	C	O	R	C

ANACONDA   JAGUAR   CROCODILE   HONEY BADGER
HARPY EAGLE   DUNG BEETLE   WOLVERINE   GRIZZLY BEAR
TIGER   SPOTTED HYENA

PORTRAIT OF A PREDATOR: SALTWATER CROCODILE

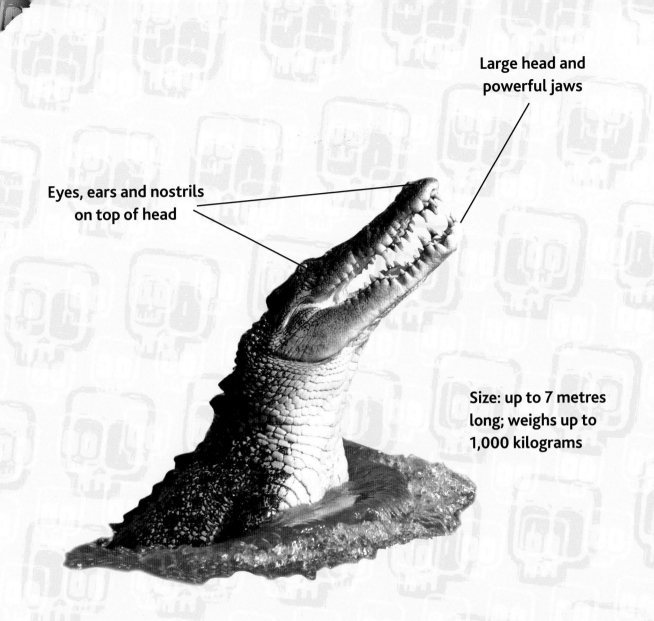

Large head and powerful jaws

Eyes, ears and nostrils on top of head

Size: up to 7 metres long; weighs up to 1,000 kilograms

The largest of all the crocodiles, the saltwater crocodile has a hugely powerful bite. This awesome hunter spends most of its time in the water where it lies watching for prey, with only its eyes and nose visible above the surface. It attacks anything from crabs and turtles to wild boar and buffalo, killing its victims with a single snap of its toothy jaws.

Steve and the Deadly team tried to measure the strength of a 'Saltie's' bite using a special bite pressure gauge. On the first go, the crocodile gave the gauge a brief nip and that measured a mighty 1,200 pounds per square inch. On the next try, the crocodile bit with such force that it tore the gauge away and destroyed it completely. In other trials the 'Saltie' registered an amazing 3,700 pounds per square inch. In comparison, a human bite is about 150–200 pounds per square inch.

This crocodile lives in southern India, Southeast Asia and Australia, and males can grow up to 6 or 7 metres long – that's longer than most family cars.

CHAPTER 7
DEADLY VENOM

The **creatures** in this chapter all use deadly venom to kill or **paralyse** their prey or to **defend** themselves. There is a **difference** between **poisonous** animals

and **venomous** animals. A venomous animal delivers its **toxins** to the animal with a **bite**, **spine**, fang or other device. A **poisonous** animal must be **touched** or **eaten** by the other creature.

DEADLY VENOM FACTS

Tiny but deadly, the **BLUE-RINGED OCTOPUS** is one of the most venomous of all sea creatures. It preys on crabs and small fish, which it bites with its parrot-like beak while injecting very powerful venom. The bite can cause paralysis in humans and can be extremely dangerous.

Normally this little creature is brownish in colour, but if it's disturbed or threatened bright blue rings appear all over its body – a warning to enemies to stay well away.

Tentacles up to 3 metres long trail from the bell-shaped body of the **BOX JELLYFISH**. The bell is only about 25 centimetres across but this creature is a highly venomous predator. Its tentacles are covered with thousands of stinging cells that can fire off venom to kill or paralyse prey such as fish and shrimp.

Unlike most jellyfish, which just float with the ocean currents, the box jellyfish is able to swim at speeds of about 7 kilometres an hour.

Bright colours are often a sign that an animal is venomous, and this is certainly true of the **YELLOW SEA SNAKE**. This ocean-living reptile grows up to 1.8 metres long and has a yellow body marked with bold black rings. It hunts fish, which it kills with a venomous bite from its fangs.

Right at the end of a **SCORPION**'s body is a sharp, curved sting linked to a pair of venom glands. The scorpion can swing this over its body and plunge it into another creature, delivering a venomous sting to defend itself against attack or to kill or paralyse large prey. The scorpion may sometimes just grasp smaller prey in its large pincers without stinging.

All scorpions have a sting but not all are deadly. Only a few are dangerous to humans.

The **GILA MONSTER** grows to as much as 58 centimetres long and is the largest lizard in North America. It eats rats, mice, birds, eggs and other lizards but can go for months without food, as it can store fat in its broad tail. It has venomous saliva, which it may use to defend itself, but is also thought to help digest its prey.

CONE SNAILS have a prettily patterned shell but contain a deadly venom. Only about 15 centimetres long, the snail has venom powerful enough to kill people. The snail glides slowly over the ocean floor searching for fish, worms or even other snails to eat. A tube-like structure called a proboscis extends from its shell and from this it can fire a deadly harpoon containing more types of toxin than the venom of any other creature. This paralyses the prey and the snail then engulfs it and swallows it whole.

SYDNEY FUNNEL-WEB SPIDERS are among the most dangerous of all spiders. They live in burrows that they line with silk they spin from their own bodies. Females spend most of their lives in their burrow, only popping out to catch passing insects and small animals such as lizards and frogs, which they kill with a venomous bite. Males often leave the burrow at night to hunt and to search for a mate.

A massive fish, the **STINGRAY** measures up to 2 metres across. It spends much of its time half buried in sand in the sea bed, where it finds prey such as clams, worms and small fish. It has a long spine at the end of its tail which can deliver a venomous wound, but the stingray generally uses its venom to defend itself, not to kill prey. If stepped on by an unwary swimmer, the stingray whips its tail up to drive its stinging spine into the intruder.

66

DEADLY VENOM WORDSEARCH

All the animals in this puzzle have deadly venom they use to attack prey or defend themselves. Can you find their names?

B	H	R	D	X	A	W	Y	Q	I	O	X	Z	T	F
B	J	A	R	Q	T	N	L	V	Y	X	O	T	U	X
Y	A	R	G	N	I	T	S	K	J	U	O	N	D	D
R	T	B	X	I	V	Z	Y	C	F	C	N	Z	Z	A
S	E	G	H	S	I	F	Y	L	L	E	J	X	O	B
Q	A	T	V	L	X	A	S	G	L	A	A	Y	S	M
O	Q	Z	S	X	G	Z	S	W	A	L	A	E	U	A
O	M	M	T	N	G	U	E	C	I	N	A	E	P	M
K	I	N	G	C	O	B	R	A	O	S	O	N	O	K
W	Q	R	V	X	S	M	N	R	N	R	H	Z	T	C
V	I	S	A	P	D	S	A	A	K	P	P	Z	C	A
N	L	W	I	F	E	X	K	L	L	W	W	I	O	L
N	C	D	O	N	V	E	P	K	I	N	S	Z	O	B
E	E	L	O	H	J	D	Q	X	H	G	A	B	N	N
R	X	C	C	H	P	O	W	G	N	A	X	G	D	B

OCTOPUS　　**SEA SNAKE**　　**KING COBRA**　　**STINGRAY**
GILA MONSTER　　**SCORPION**　　**BLACK MAMBA**　　**FUNNEL-WEB SPIDER**
CONE SNAIL　　**BOX JELLYFISH**

PORTRAIT OF A PREDATOR: KING COBRA

At up to 5.5 metres, the king cobra is the longest of all venomous snakes. It moves swiftly over the ground as it hunts for prey, usually other snakes, which it kills with its venomous bite. Although the king cobra's venom is not as powerful as that of some other snakes, it produces a lot of it and delivers enough in a single bite to kill an elephant or as many as 20 people. The venom affects the victim's nervous system and can stop it breathing.

If threatened, the king cobra lifts the front third of its body off the ground. It spreads the hood of skin on its head to make itself look even larger and fiercer than it is, while hissing or 'growling' loudly to warn off the enemy.

King cobras generally live in mangrove swamps, rainforests and woodlands in parts of Asia from India and southern China to Indonesia and the Philippines. They do have a gentler side. When the female cobra is ready to lay her eggs, she makes a nest of twigs and dead leaves. She lays her eggs in this nest, covers them with more leaves and then curls up on top to guard them from predators. Even newly hatched king cobras have a venomous bite.

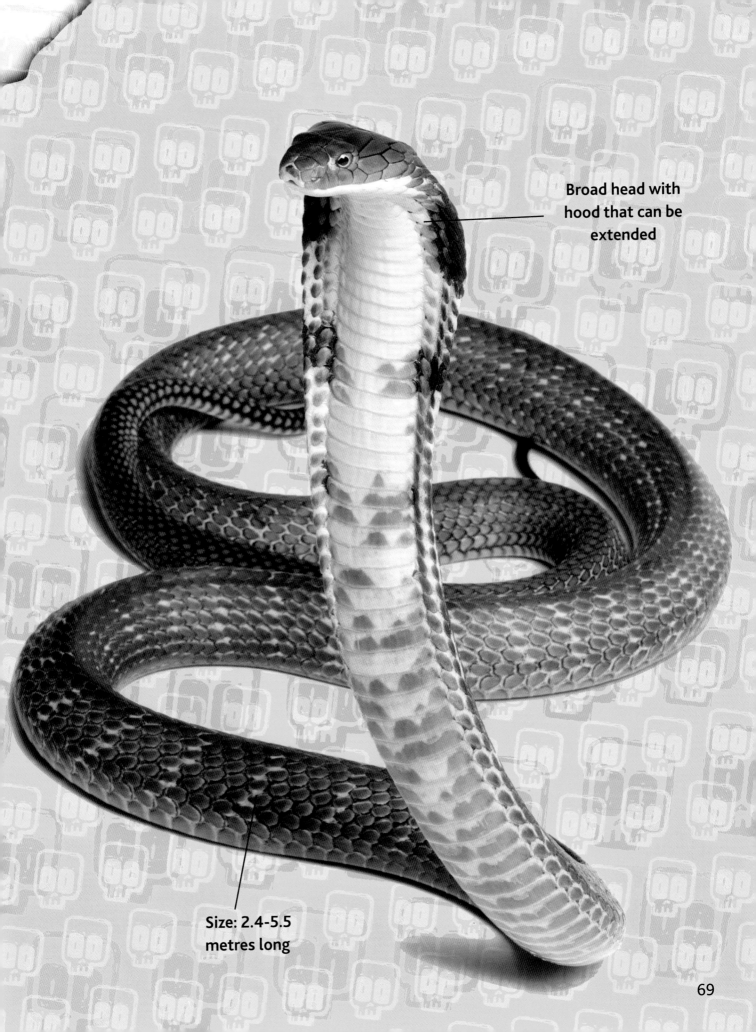

Broad head with hood that can be extended

Size: 2.4-5.5 metres long

DEADLY 60 QUIZ

Now have a look at our Deadly quiz. The answers are all somewhere in this book so you'll be able to get them all right!

1 Which is the fastest-running bird?
a Ostrich
b Roadrunner

2 What is the turkey vulture's most important sense?
a Smell
b Hearing
c Sight

3 Which is the biggest big cat?
a Jaguar
b Lion
c Siberian tiger

4 Which is the longest venomous snake?
a Rattlesnake
b King cobra
c Black mamba

5 How long can an African elephant's tusks grow?
a 3.5 metres
b 2 metres
c 50 centimetres

6 Where do poison dart frogs live?
a Africa
b Australia
c Central and South America

10 What does a golden eagle use to kill its prey?
a Sharp talons
b Hooked beak

11 Where is the stingray's sting?
a On its head
b On its tail
c On its fins

12 What kind of trap does an antlion make?
a Web
b Pit
c Burrow

7 What kind of animal is a margay?
a Cat
b Lizard
c Fish

8 What does the assassin bug like to eat?
a Fruit
b Worms
c Spiders

9 Which mammal has the thickest coat?
a Sea otter
b Polar bear
c Wolf

PUZZLE ANSWERS

Here you will find all the answers to the puzzles shown in this book. Have fun . . .

p17 DEADLY TRICKS WORDSEARCH

R	N	U	T	T	M	W	V	M	P	U	N	G	R	H
E	F	O	W	W	O	P	A	E	Y	R	L	K	S	A
D	I	M	R	B	Q	R	U	M	N	B	K	I	Z	C
D	R	F	U	E	G	B	J	Z	U	O	F	T	A	B
A	E	B	I	A	H	R	B	T	Z	R	S	N	N	Q
H	F	N	Y	X	Q	N	J	E	E	B	T	F	E	M
T	L	R	S	B	A	X	E	L	G	I	A	K	L	S
A	Y	P	Z	C	R	Y	G	E	L	O	F	Q	M	M
E	D	T	O	D	U	N	H	V	R	B	N	U	Q	I
D	B	M	S	Z	A	A	I	D	I	G	W	G	O	I
R	E	G	D	A	B	P	Q	H	F	Q	F	O	W	T
S	H	L	M	E	E	A	L	L	I	G	A	T	O	R
J	R	G	E	R	W	B	N	K	K	A	A	Q	N	M
G	U	B	N	I	S	S	A	S	S	A	O	R	O	Y
S	V	Q	R	D	G	W	T	T	Z	Z	P	R	Y	B

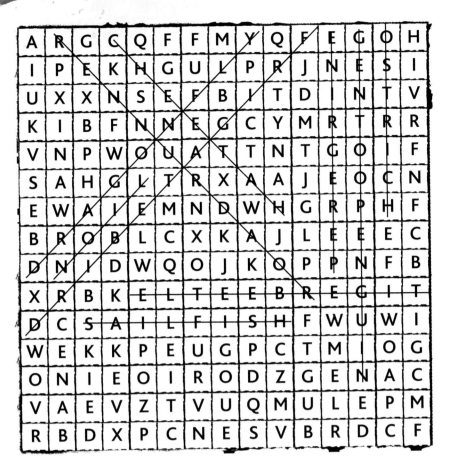

A	R	G	C	Q	F	F	M	Y	Q	F	E	G	O	H	
I	P	E	K	H	G	U	L	P	R	J	N	E	S	I	
U	X	X	N	S	E	F	B	I	T	D	I	N	T	V	
K	I	B	F	N	N	E	G	C	Y	M	R	T	R	R	
V	N	P	W	O	U	A	T	T	N	T	G	O	I	F	
S	A	H	G	L	T	R	X	A	A	J	E	O	C	N	
E	W	A	I	E	M	N	D	W	H	G	R	P	H	F	
B	R	O	B	L	C	X	K	A	J	L	E	E	E	C	
D	N	I	D	W	Q	O	J	K	O	P	P	N	F	B	
X	R	B	K	E	L	T	E	E	B	R	E	G	I	T	
D	C	S	A	I	L	F	I	S	H	F	W	U	W	I	
W	E	K	K	P	E	U	G	P	C	T	M	I	O	G	
O	N	I	E	O	I	R	O	D	Z	G	E	N	A	C	
V	A	E	V	Z	T	V	U	Q	M	U	L	E	P	M	
R	B	D	X	P	C	N	E	S	V	B	R	D	C	F	

P	Y	B	Y	V	B	P	S	D	K	E	O	I	P	O
Y	R	C	T	V	E	J	F	U	T	T	A	M	R	S
W	E	O	C	T	J	A	J	I	P	S	Y	E	Y	X
F	D	R	G	H	S	O	K	E	M	O	D	B	F	A
V	I	A	T	L	I	V	E	Q	C	I	T	Z	H	Q
I	P	N	T	W	R	M	E	O	P	S	T	C	I	U
L	S	G	G	N	B	H	P	S	E	Z	U	H	Q	S
E	R	U	T	L	U	V	N	A	I	T	P	Y	G	E
L	O	T	L	I	W	E	O	M	N	G	R	Y	I	G
C	O	A	Q	R	D	T	T	J	R	Z	D	T	W	I
A	D	N	R	R	T	N	B	Y	X	J	E	M	O	F
Q	P	R	A	E	N	O	I	L	T	N	A	E	R	C
Y	A	G	R	Z	J	Z	K	H	L	C	K	Q	C	S
S	R	O	K	Y	I	A	J	G	M	Q	L	N	G	V
N	T	J	W	A	T	E	R	S	P	I	D	E	R	P

DEADLY SENSES WORDSEARCH

```
E R M E O G W R L R T G F D A
V R I R G E Y R K A O O E X U
P A U T W B K B Y E O N A C L
Q O S T V D F C L B I Y W C V
X V X P L I I K P R H I S D V
M K H P U U P R G A Q W M O P
H G R O U O V E V L S U N G L
Q T R A Y E R Y R O V O R Y A
J A Y J H E Q X E P K E V C T
X L X I P S E A I K Y A L P Y
L W O N R A B V D S R N D W P
G P X Y D E U T E N U U Q I U
B G E L E P H A N T W M T W S
N M D R P T L D O N K K H I D
M K T R K N A A C K P T S K I
```

p51 DEADLY WEAPONS WORDSEARCH

```
T N A W A J P A R T G X S E T
S K S A A B C B I T U I E Y N
G D K H X N G W E T O L A B
E Q S O O G E J E N J N E E S
A Q L I S R E T A O H Y C Y E
B W L D S L J M N P A Z T A C
Q K H H E Q G G Q W A Y Z R W N
F V A M A M T I S S H R I M P
Q R N L I S E R V N L P C R J
K S Z Y H E N A D H D E E Y U
T X A D E F Z R G Q V L E L W
Q R W A S P J N N L A E L F E
P K Y B W W O Q I X E C A G J
O N K G B U R P V C X J K C G
P X H T Y T N Y F P Y Y Q J W
```

H	E	T	X	C	D	K	T	Q	E	G	A	L	F	U
A	N	N	I	O	M	I	H	P	P	N	P	Z	E	I
R	I	G	M	G	D	K	S	L	E	M	Y	L	D	J
P	R	J	R	T	E	F	V	Y	J	A	G	U	A	R
Y	E	B	M	I	N	R	H	K	Y	A	N	K	J	B
E	V	E	C	M	Z	D	A	A	Q	G	U	G	L	M
A	L	C	F	C	E	Z	D	J	B	J	R	B	P	K
G	O	N	S	T	Y	N	L	E	L	M	E	A	G	H
L	W	B	T	H	O	N	E	Y	B	A	D	G	E	R
E	Q	O	V	C	O	T	R	U	B	T	P	F	O	N
L	P	N	A	I	L	L	K	T	J	E	F	Q	P	P
S	R	N	A	E	K	P	R	H	Y	W	A	H	N	G
H	A	I	Q	M	A	Z	K	N	K	T	M	R	H	H
T	X	W	K	D	Q	G	L	R	P	Z	R	V	Q	N
N	A	Z	D	A	W	E	L	I	D	O	C	O	R	C

p59
DEADLY POWER & STRENGTH WORDSEARCH

p67 DEADLY VENOM WORDSEARCH

B	H	R	D	X	A	W	Y	Q	I	O	X	Z	T	F
B	J	A	R	Q	T	N	L	V	Y	X	O	T	U	X
Y	A	R	G	N	I	T	S	K	J	U	O	N	D	D
R	T	B	X	I	V	Z	Y	C	F	C	N	Z	Z	A
S	E	G	H	S	I	F	Y	L	L	E	J	X	O	B
Q	A	T	V	L	X	A	S	G	L	A	A	Y	S	M
O	Q	Z	S	X	G	Z	S	W	A	L	A	E	U	A
O	M	M	T	N	G	U	E	C	I	N	A	E	P	M
K	I	N	G	C	O	B	R	A	O	S	O	N	O	K
W	Q	R	V	X	S	M	N	R	N	R	H	Z	T	C
V	I	S	A	P	D	S	A	A	K	P	R	Z	C	A
N	L	W	I	F	E	X	K	L	L	W	W	I	O	L
N	C	D	O	N	V	E	P	K	I	N	S	Z	Q	B
E	E	L	O	H	J	D	Q	X	H	G	A	B	N	N
R	X	C	C	H	P	O	W	G	N	A	X	G	D	B

p70
DEADLY 60 QUIZ
1 a; 2 a; 3 c; 4 b; 5 a; 6 c; 7 a;
8 c; 9 a; 10 a; 11 b; 12 b

Follow in STEVE BACKSHALL's footsteps with these deluxe DEADLY Gift Books:

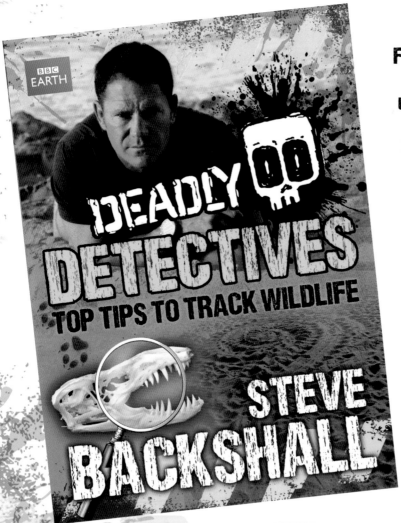

Finding **wildlife** is rarely easy — unless you're **Steve Backshall!** In DEADLY DETECTIVES Steve tells **young** trackers **everything** they need to **know** about the origins of tracking, what you **need** to become a tracker and how to do it, whether the **wild** world is your own back **garden**, ancient woodlands, the **riverside** or **coast**.

Don't miss **Steve Backshall**'s incredible first-hand account of his **14-month** voyage from the **Arctic** to the **Antarctic** via Alaska, California, Hawaii, Mexico and Brazil and **many** more **amazing** locations besides. It's the **DEADLY** adventure of a lifetime.

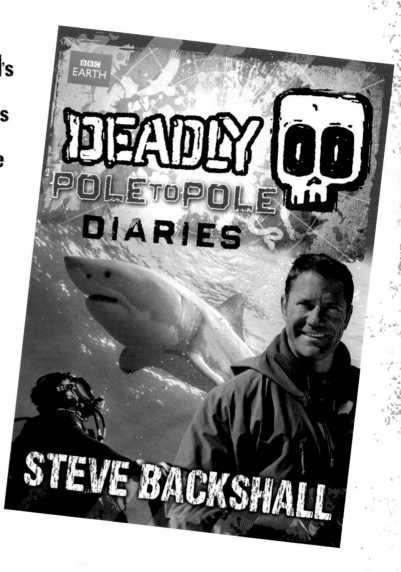

JOIN THE DEADLY ADVENTURE!